Contents

T0055926

Piece no.		Page no.
1	Hark! the herald-angels sing	4
2	The holly and the ivy	6
3	Ding dong! merrily on high	8
4	Andrew mine, Jasper mine	10
5	Silent night	12
6	I saw three ships	11
7	O little town of Bethlehem	14
8	Once in royal David's city	15
9	Go tell it on the mountain	16
10	We wish you a merry Christmas	17
11	Shepherds watched	18
12	O Christmas tree	19
13	We three kings	20
14	Bethl'em lay a-sleeping	22
15	Good King Wenceslas	23
16	Infant holy, infant lowly	24
17	Deck the hall	25
18	O come, all ye faithful	26
19	Away in a manger	28
20	The first Nowell	29
21	Zither Carol	30
22	God rest you merry, gentlemen	31
23	Skaters' Waltz	32
24	Dance of the Reed Pipes	33
25	While shepherds watched their flocks	34
26	Children, go!	35
27	Child in a manger	36
28	Jingle, bells	38
29	Mary had a baby	39
30	Christmas Calypso	40
31	Hogmanay Reel	42
32	Auld Lang Syne	43

1. Hark! the herald-angels sing

Felix Mendelssohn (1809–47)

© Oxford University Press 2010. Photocopying this copyright material is ILLEGAL.

OXFORD
UNIVERSITY PRESS

Cello Time Christmas

piano accompaniment book

Kathy and David Blackwell

OXFORD
UNIVERSITY PRESS

Great Clarendon Street, Oxford OX2 6DP, England

Oxford University Press is a department of the University of Oxford.
It furthers the University's aim of excellence in research, scholarship,
and education by publishing worldwide

Oxford is a registered trade mark of Oxford University Press
in the UK and in certain other countries

This collection © Oxford University Press 2010

Kathy and David Blackwell have asserted their Moral Rights under the Copyright,
Designs and Patents Act, 1988

Database right Oxford University Press (maker)

First published 2010

All rights reserved. No part of this publication may be reproduced, stored in a
retrieval system, or transmitted, in any form or by any means, without the prior
permission in writing of Oxford University Press, or as expressly permitted by law.
Enquiries concerning reproduction outside the scope of the above should be sent
to the Music Copyright Department, Oxford University Press, at the address above

Permission to perform these works in public (except in the course of
divine worship) should normally be obtained from the Performing Right Society Ltd
(PRS), 29/33 Berners Street, London W1T 3AB, or its affiliated Societies in each country
throughout the world, unless the owner or the occupier of the premises
being used holds a licence from the Society

Permission to make a recording must be obtained in advance for the Mechanical-
Copyright Protection Society Ltd (MCPS), Elgar House, 41 Streatham High Road,
London SW16 1ER, or its affiliated Societies in each country throughout the world

ISBN 978-0-19-337225-2

Music and text origination by
Barnes Music Engraving Ltd, East Sussex
Printed in Great Britain on acid-free paper by
Caligraving Ltd, Thetford, Norfolk.

Teacher's note

In Nos. 3, 7, 8, 15, 16, and 17, sections that are presented as repeats in the cello book are written out in the accompaniment.

f
Joy - ful all ye na - tions rise, Join the tri - umph
f
of the skies, With th'an - gel - ic host pro - claim,
Christ is born in Beth - le - hem. Hark! the he - rald -
ff
ff
- an - gels sing Glo - ry to the new - born King.

2. The holly and the ivy

English trad.

© Oxford University Press 2010. Photocopying this copyright material is ILLEGAL.

f
hol - ly bears the crown. The ris - ing of the
mf
mf
sun And the run - ning of the deer, The
play - ing of the mer - ry or - gan, Sweet sing - ing in the choir.

3. Ding dong! merrily on high

16th-century French melody

© Oxford University Press 2010. Photocopying this copyright material is ILLEGAL.

f
Glo - - - - - - - - - - -
f
- - - - - ri - a, Ho - san - na in ex - cel - sis!
Glo - - - - - - - - - - -
- - - - - ri - a, Ho - san - na in ex - cel - sis!

4. Andrew mine, Jasper mine

Moravian carol

Music: © Oxford University Press 2010. Words by C. K. Offer from *Three Moravian Carols* © Oxford University Press 1962.
Reproduced by permission of Oxford University Press. Photocopying this copyright material is ILLEGAL.

5. Silent night
next page

6. I saw three ships

English trad.

Nos. 5 and 6 have been reversed to avoid a page turn.

© Oxford University Press 2010. Photocopying this copyright material is ILLEGAL.

5. Silent night

Franz Gruber (1787–1863)

© Oxford University Press 2010. Photocopying this copyright material is ILLEGAL.

Round yon vir - gin mo - ther and child.
Ho - ly in - fant so ten - der and mild,
mf
Sleep in hea - ven - ly peace,
mf
mp
Sleep in hea - ven - ly peace.
mp

7. O little town of Bethlehem

English trad.

© Oxford University Press 2010. Photocopying this copyright material is ILLEGAL.

8. Once in royal David's city

H. J. Gauntlett (1805–76)

© Oxford University Press 2010. Photocopying this copyright material is ILLEGAL.

9. Go tell it on the mountain

© Oxford University Press 2010. Photocopying this copyright material is ILLEGAL.

10. We wish you a merry Christmas

trad. West Country

© Oxford University Press 2010. Photocopying this copyright material is ILLEGAL.

11. Shepherds watched

© Oxford University Press 2010. Photocopying this copyright material is ILLEGAL.

12. O Christmas tree

© Oxford University Press 2010. Photocopying this copyright material is ILLEGAL.

13. We three kings

J. H. Hopkins (1820–91)

© Oxford University Press 2010. Photocopying this copyright material is ILLEGAL.

f
star of won - der, star of night,
f starry!
Star with roy - al beau - ty bright,
West - ward lead - ing, still pro - ceed - ing,
Guide us to thy per - fect light.

14. Bethl'em lay a-sleeping

Polish carol

© Oxford University Press 2010. Photocopying this copyright material is ILLEGAL.

15. Good King Wenceslas

© Oxford University Press 2010. Photocopying this copyright material is ILLEGAL.

16. Infant holy, infant lowly

Polish carol

© Oxford University Press 2010. Photocopying this copyright material is ILLEGAL.

17. Deck the hall

© Oxford University Press 2010. Photocopying this copyright material is ILLEGAL.

18. O come, all ye faithful

J. F. Wade (*c.*1711–86)

© Oxford University Press 2010. Photocopying this copyright material is ILLEGAL.

f
mp
Come and be - hold him Born the King of An - gels: O
f
mp
mf
f
come, let us a - dore him, O come, let us a - dore him, O
mf
f
come, let us a - dore him, Christ the Lord!

19. Away in a manger

William J. Kirkpatrick (1838–1921)

© Oxford University Press 2010. Photocopying this copyright material is ILLEGAL.

20. The first Nowell

© Oxford University Press 2010. Photocopying this copyright material is ILLEGAL.

21. Zither Carol

Czech carol

© Oxford University Press 2010. Photocopying this copyright material is ILLEGAL.

22. God rest you merry, gentlemen

© Oxford University Press 2010. Photocopying this copyright material is ILLEGAL.

23. Skaters' Waltz

Emil Waldteufel (1837–1915)

Cello parts swap round on repeat. In the cello book the repeat is written out.

© Oxford University Press 2010. Photocopying this copyright material is ILLEGAL.

24. Dance of the Reed Pipes

(from the *Nutcracker* ballet)

Pyotr Ilyich Tchaikovsky (1840–93)

© Oxford University Press 2010. Photocopying this copyright material is ILLEGAL.

25. While shepherds watched their flocks

Este's Psalter (1592)

© Oxford University Press 2010. Photocopying this copyright material is ILLEGAL.

26. Children, go!

© Oxford University Press 2010. Photocopying this copyright material is ILLEGAL.

27. Child in a manger

Celtic trad.

© Oxford University Press 2010. Photocopying this copyright material is ILLEGAL.

mf
ho - ly and mild; Sent from the high - -
mp
mf
mp
- est, Come down in glo - - ry; Tell the glad
p
mp
sto - - ry, Wel - come the child.
p

28. Jingle, bells

J. Pierpont (1822–93)

© Oxford University Press 2010. Photocopying this copyright material is ILLEGAL.

29. Mary had a baby

American trad.

© Oxford University Press 2010. Photocopying this copyright material is ILLEGAL.

30. Christmas Calypso

Kathy & David Blackwell

© Oxford University Press 2004 and 2010. Photocopying this copyright material is ILLEGAL.

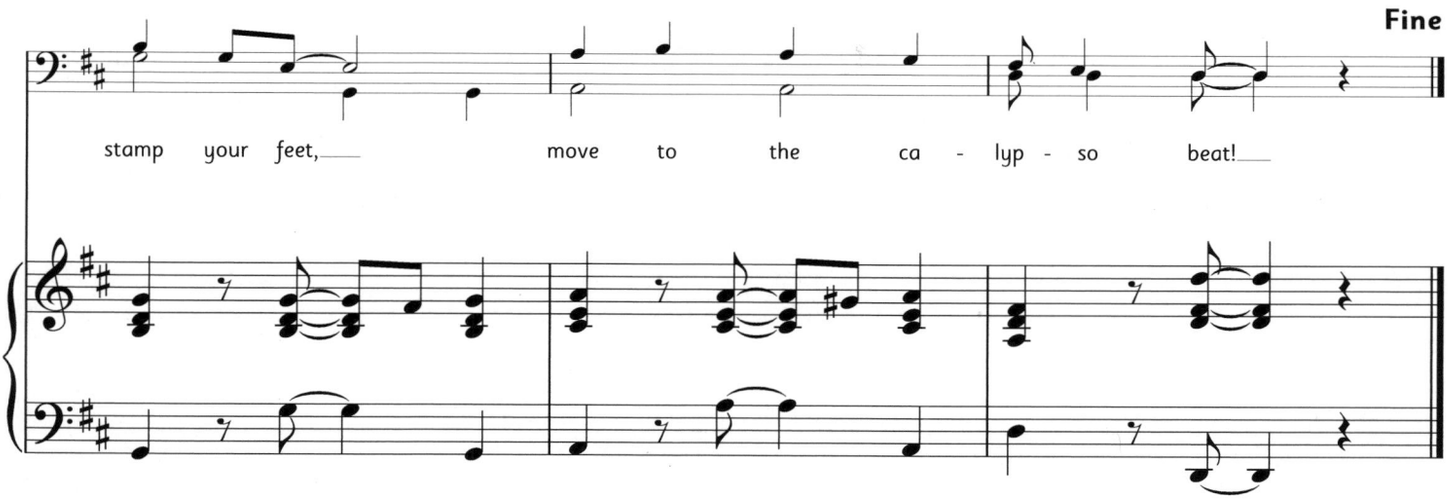
Fine
stamp your feet, move to the ca - lyp - so beat!

mf
Way back in Beth - le - hem, in a sim - ple sta - ble,
mf

D.𝄋. al Fine
Je - sus, that ba - by boy, came to save us all! So dance the

31. Hogmanay Reel

Kathy & David Blackwell

© Oxford University Press 2001 and 2010. Photocopying this copyright material is ILLEGAL.

32. Auld Lang Syne

© Oxford University Press 2010. Photocopying this copyright material is ILLEGAL.

Cello Time Christmas

piano accompaniment book

Cello Time is a great series for young cellists. Packed with lively original tunes, easy duets, and traditional pieces, the books are carefully paced and organized to build confidence every step of the way. With plenty of entertaining illustrations and audio to play along to, with **Cello Time** it really is fun to play!

Cello Time
by Kathy and David Blackwell

Cello Time Joggers (a first book of very easy pieces)	cello book with audio piano accompaniment book
Cello Time Runners (a second book of easy pieces)	cello book with audio piano accompaniment book
Cello Time Sprinters (a third book of pieces)	cello book with audio piano accompaniment book
Cello Time Christmas (a stockingful of 32 easy pieces)	cello book with audio piano accompaniment book

BLACKWELL Cello Time Christmas ***Piano Book***

Cover illustration by Alan Rowe

OXFORD
UNIVERSITY PRESS

www.oup.com

ISBN 978-0-19-337225-2

9 780193 372252